150 DAYS OF Growing in Gratitude
A JOURNAL

By: Alexandra Elle

Illustrated by: Josefina Sanders

Dear Journaler,

The *Growing in Gratitude* journal was created to support you in pausing, reflecting, and tapping into the personal practice of gratefulness. For 150 days, keep this journal by your bed or in your bag and dive into strengthening the appreciation for who you are, what you have, and how you can serve others. Life and time are fleeting. As you write in these pages, I encourage you to lean into mindfulness by rooting deeply and intentionally into your present moments. Give thanks for who and where you are in life, even if it seems to be a difficult task. Remind yourself that every day you rise is another chance to start over, become better, and show up for not only yourself but also those around you. I hope these pages serve as a form of therapy and offer clarity as you write and explore the gratitude you have for your current journey and the one ahead.

With love,

xoxo

In all that you do, give the gift of gratitude.

Today I am grateful for: USE THESE LINES FOR GRATITUDE EXPRESSION!

1. My forgiving heart. Its resilience offers hope.

2. the journey ahead and lessons to come.

3. growth. I've come a long way, and I'm proud!

Today's intention:

USE THIS BOX TO DOODLE OR WRITE get creative!

To nurture the parts of me that need more love

USE THESE LINES TO REFLECT ON YOUR OFFERINGS TO THE WORLD.

Because I have _a big heart_, I will give _love to others_.

Day _1 or date_ KEEP TRACK OF YOUR STARTING POINT.

Today I am grateful for:

1. _____

2. _____

3. _____

Today's intention:

Because I have _____ , I will give _____

Day _____

Today I am grateful for:

1. _____

2. _____

3. _____

Today's intention:

```
┌─────────────────────────────────────────────┐
│                                               │
│                                               │
│                                               │
│                                               │
│                                               │
│                                               │
│                                               │
└─────────────────────────────────────────────┘
```

Because I have _____ , I will give _____

Day _____

Today I am grateful for:

1. _____

2. _____

3. _____

Today's intention:

Because I have _____, I will give _____.

Day _____

Today I am grateful for:

1. _____

2. _____

3. _____

Today's intention:

```
┌─────────────────────────────────────────┐
│                                           │
│                                           │
│                                           │
│                                           │
│                                           │
│                                           │
│                                           │
│                                           │
│                                           │
└─────────────────────────────────────────┘
```

Because I have _____ , I will give _____

Day _____

Today I am grateful for:

1. _____

2. _____

3. _____

Today's intention:

Because I have _____, I will give _____.

Day _____

Today I am grateful for:

1. _____

2. _____

3. _____

Today's intention:

```

```

Because I have _____, I will give _____.

Day _____

Today I am grateful for:

1. _____

2. _____

3. _____

Today's intention:

Because I have _____, I will give _____

Day _____

Today I am grateful for:

1. _____

2. _____

3. _____

Today's intention:

Because I have _____ , I will give _____

Day _____

Today I am grateful for:

1. _____

2. _____

3. _____

Today's intention:

Because I have _____, I will give _____.

Day _____

Today I am grateful for:

1. _____

2. _____

3. _____

Today's intention:

```

```

Because I have _____, I will give _____.

Day _____

Today I am grateful for:

1. _____

2. _____

3. _____

Today's intention:

_____

Because I have _____ , I will give _____ .

Day _____

Today I am grateful for:

1. _____

2. _____

3. _____

Today's intention:

| |
| |

Because I have _____ , I will give _____

Day _____

Today I am grateful for:

1. _____

2. _____

3. _____

Today's intention:

```
┌─────────────────────────────────────┐
│                                       │
│                                       │
│                                       │
│                                       │
│                                       │
│                                       │
└─────────────────────────────────────┘
```

Because I have _____ , I will give _____

Day _____

Today I am grateful for:

1. _____

2. _____

3. _____

Today's intention:

```



```

Because I have _____ , I will give _____

Day _____

Today I am grateful for:

1. _____

2. _____

3. _____

Today's intention:

Because I have _____ , I will give _____.

Day _____

Today I am grateful for:

1. _____

2. _____

3. _____

Today's intention:

_____

Because I have _____ , I will give _____

Day _____

Today I am grateful for:

1. _____

2. _____

3. _____

Today's intention:

Because I have _____, I will give _____.

Day _____

Today I am grateful for:

1. _____

2. _____

3. _____

Today's intention:

_____

Because I have _____, I will give _____

Day _____

Today I am grateful for:

1. _____

2. _____

3. _____

Today's intention:

Because I have _____, I will give _____.

Day _____

Today I am grateful for:

1. _____

2. _____

3. _____

Today's intention:

_____

Because I have _____ , I will give _____

Day _____

Today I am grateful for:

1. _____

2. _____

3. _____

Today's intention:

Because I have _____ , I will give _____ .

Day _____

Today I am grateful for:

1. _____

2. _____

3. _____

Today's intention:

Because I have _____, I will give _____.

Day _____

Today I am grateful for:

1. _____

2. _____

3. _____

Today's intention:

```



```

Because I have _____ , I will give _____

Day _____

Today I am grateful for:

1. _____

2. _____

3. _____

Today's intention:

┌───┐
│   │
│   │
│   │
│   │
│   │
│   │
│   │
└───┘

Because I have _____ , I will give _____

Day _____

Today I am grateful for:

1. _____

2. _____

3. _____

Today's intention:

Because I have _____, I will give _____.

Day _____

Today I am grateful for:

1. _____

2. _____

3. _____

Today's intention:

```
┌──────────────────────────────────────────────┐
│                                                │
│                                                │
│                                                │
│                                                │
│                                                │
│                                                │
│                                                │
│                                                │
│                                                │
└──────────────────────────────────────────────┘
```

Because I have _____ , I will give _____

Day _____

Today I am grateful for:

1. _____

2. _____

3. _____

Today's intention:

```
┌─────────────────────────────────────────┐
│                                         │
│                                         │
│                                         │
│                                         │
│                                         │
│                                         │
│                                         │
└─────────────────────────────────────────┘
```

Because I have _____, I will give _____

Day _____

Today I am grateful for:

1. _____

2. _____

3. _____

Today's intention:

```
┌─────────────────────────────────────────────────┐
│                                                   │
│                                                   │
│                                                   │
│                                                   │
│                                                   │
│                                                   │
│                                                   │
└─────────────────────────────────────────────────┘
```

Because I have _____ , I will give _____

Day _____

Today I am grateful for:

1. _____

2. _____

3. _____

Today's intention:

```
┌──────────────────────────────────────┐
│                                        │
│                                        │
│                                        │
│                                        │
│                                        │
│                                        │
│                                        │
│                                        │
└──────────────────────────────────────┘
```

Because I have _____, I will give _____.

Day _____

Today I am grateful for:

1. _____

2. _____

3. _____

Today's intention:

┌───┐
│   │
│   │
│   │
│   │
│   │
└───┘

Because I have _____, I will give _____

Day _____

Today I am grateful for:

1. _____

2. _____

3. _____

Today's intention:

Because I have _____, I will give _____

Day _____

Today I am grateful for:

1. _____

2. _____

3. _____

Today's intention:

Because I have _____, I will give _____.

Day _____

Today I am grateful for:

1. _____

2. _____

3. _____

Today's intention:

[ ]

Because I have _____, I will give _____.

Day _____

Today I am grateful for:

1. _____

2. _____

3. _____

Today's intention:

```



```

Because I have _____ , I will give _____

Day _____

Today I am grateful for:

1. _____

2. _____

3. _____

Today's intention:

_____

Because I have _____ , I will give _____ .

Day _____

Today I am grateful for:

1. _____

2. _____

3. _____

Today's intention:

[ ]

Because I have _____ , I will give _____

Day _____

Today I am grateful for:

1. _____

2. _____

3. _____

Today's intention:

_____

Because I have _____ , I will give _____

Day _____

Today I am grateful for:

1. _____

2. _____

3. _____

Today's intention:

```
+--------------------------------------------------+
|                                                  |
|                                                  |
|                                                  |
|                                                  |
|                                                  |
|                                                  |
+--------------------------------------------------+
```

Because I have _____ , I will give _____

Day _____

Today I am grateful for:

1. _____

2. _____

3. _____

Today's intention:

Because I have _____ , I will give _____

Day _____

Today I am grateful for:

1. _____

2. _____

3. _____

Today's intention:

[box]

Because I have _____ , I will give _____

Day _____

Today I am grateful for:

1. _____

2. _____

3. _____

Today's intention:

Because I have _____ , I will give _____ .

Day _____

Today I am grateful for:

1. _____

2. _____

3. _____

Today's intention:

```


```

Because I have _____ , I will give _____

Day _____

Today I am grateful for:

1. _____

2. _____

3. _____

Today's intention:

```



```

Because I have _____, I will give _____

Day _____

Today I am grateful for:

1. _____

2. _____

3. _____

Today's intention:

```



```

Because I have _____ , I will give _____ .

Day _____

Today I am grateful for:

1. _____

2. _____

3. _____

Today's intention:

[ ]

Because I have _____ , I will give _____

Day _____

Today I am grateful for:

1. _____

2. _____

3. _____

Today's intention:

```
┌─────────────────────────────────────────────────┐
│                                                   │
│                                                   │
│                                                   │
│                                                   │
│                                                   │
│                                                   │
│                                                   │
└─────────────────────────────────────────────────┘
```

Because I have _____, I will give _____.

Day _____

Today I am grateful for:

1. _____

2. _____

3. _____

Today's intention:

```
┌─────────────────────────────────────────┐
│                                           │
│                                           │
│                                           │
│                                           │
│                                           │
│                                           │
│                                           │
└─────────────────────────────────────────┘
```

Because I have _____ , I will give _____

Day _____

Today I am grateful for:

1. _____

2. _____

3. _____

Today's intention:

Because I have _____, I will give _____

Day _____

Today I am grateful for:

1. _____

2. _____

3. _____

Today's intention:

Because I have _____, I will give _____

Day _____

Today I am grateful for:

1. _____

2. _____

3. _____

Today's intention:

Because I have _____ , I will give _____

Day _____

Today I am grateful for:

1. _____

2. _____

3. _____

Today's intention:

```
┌─────────────────────────────────────────────┐
│                                               │
│                                               │
│                                               │
│                                               │
│                                               │
│                                               │
│                                               │
└─────────────────────────────────────────────┘
```

Because I have _____ , I will give _____ .

Day _____

Today I am grateful for:

1. _____

2. _____

3. _____

Today's intention:

Because I have _____ , I will give _____

Day _____

Today I am grateful for:

1. _____

2. _____

3. _____

Today's intention:

```
┌─────────────────────────────────────────┐
│                                           │
│                                           │
│                                           │
│                                           │
│                                           │
│                                           │
│                                           │
└─────────────────────────────────────────┘
```

Because I have _____ , I will give _____

Day _____

Today I am grateful for:

1. _____

2. _____

3. _____

Today's intention:

[ ]

Because I have _____ , I will give _____ .

Day _____

Today I am grateful for:

1. _____

2. _____

3. _____

Today's intention:

[   ]

Because I have _____ , I will give _____

Day _____

Today I am grateful for:

1. _____

2. _____

3. _____

Today's intention:

Because I have _____, I will give _____.

Day _____

Today I am grateful for:

1. _____

2. _____

3. _____

Today's intention:

```
┌─────────────────────────────────────────┐
│                                           │
│                                           │
│                                           │
│                                           │
│                                           │
│                                           │
│                                           │
└─────────────────────────────────────────┘
```

Because I have _____ , I will give _____ .

Day _____

Today I am grateful for:

1. _____

2. _____

3. _____

Today's intention:

```



```

Because I have _____ , I will give _____ .

Day _____

Today I am grateful for:

1. _____

2. _____

3. _____

Today's intention:

Because I have _____ , I will give _____ .

Day _____

Today I am grateful for:

1. _____

2. _____

3. _____

Today's intention:

```
┌─────────────────────────────────────────┐
│                                         │
│                                         │
│                                         │
│                                         │
│                                         │
│                                         │
│                                         │
└─────────────────────────────────────────┘
```

Because I have _____ , I will give _____

Day _____

Today I am grateful for:

1. _____

2. _____

3. _____

Today's intention:

Because I have _____ , I will give _____ .

Day _____

Today I am grateful for:

1. _____

2. _____

3. _____

Today's intention:

Because I have _____ , I will give _____

Day _____

Today I am grateful for:

1. _____

2. _____

3. _____

Today's intention:

Because I have _____, I will give _____

Day _____

Today I am grateful for:

1. _____

2. _____

3. _____

Today's intention:

[   ]

Because I have _____ , I will give _____

Day _____

Today I am grateful for:

1. _____

2. _____

3. _____

Today's intention:

Because I have _____ , I will give _____ .

Day _____

Today I am grateful for:

1. _____

2. _____

3. _____

Today's intention:

Because I have _____ , I will give _____

Day _____

Today I am grateful for:

1. _____

2. _____

3. _____

Today's intention:

```
┌─────────────────────────────────────────────┐
│                                               │
│                                               │
│                                               │
│                                               │
│                                               │
│                                               │
│                                               │
└─────────────────────────────────────────────┘
```

Because I have _____, I will give _____.

Day _____

Today I am grateful for:

1. _____

2. _____

3. _____

Today's intention:

Because I have _____, I will give _____.

Day _____

Today I am grateful for:

1. _____

2. _____

3. _____

Today's intention:

Because I have _____ , I will give _____

Day _____

Today I am grateful for:

1. _____

2. _____

3. _____

Today's intention:

+--+
| |
| |
| |
| |
| |
| |
| |
+--+

Because I have _____ , I will give _____

Day _____

Today I am grateful for:

1. _____

2. _____

3. _____

Today's intention:

[ ]

Because I have _____ , I will give _____ .

Day _____

Today I am grateful for:

1. _____

2. _____

3. _____

Today's intention:

Because I have _____ , I will give _____

Day _____

Today I am grateful for:

1. _____

2. _____

3. _____

Today's intention:

Because I have _____ , I will give _____ .

Day _____

Today I am grateful for:

1. _____

2. _____

3. _____

Today's intention:

[ ]

Because I have _____ , I will give _____

Day ____

Today I am grateful for:

1. _____

2. _____

3. _____

Today's intention:

```


```

Because I have _____, I will give _____.

Day _____

Today I am grateful for:

1. _____

2. _____

3. _____

Today's intention:

┌───┐
│   │
│   │
│   │
│   │
│   │
│   │
│   │
└───┘

Because I have _____ , I will give _____

Day _____

Today I am grateful for:

1. _____

2. _____

3. _____

Today's intention:

```
┌─────────────────────────────────────────────┐
│                                               │
│                                               │
│                                               │
│                                               │
│                                               │
│                                               │
│                                               │
└─────────────────────────────────────────────┘
```

Because I have _____ , I will give _____

Day _____

Today I am grateful for:

1. _____

2. _____

3. _____

Today's intention:

Because I have _____ , I will give _____

Day _____

Today I am grateful for:

1. _____

2. _____

3. _____

Today's intention:

Because I have _____ , I will give _____ .

Day _____

Today I am grateful for:

1. _____

2. _____

3. _____

Today's intention:

Because I have _____ , I will give _____

Day _____

Today I am grateful for:

1. _____

2. _____

3. _____

Today's intention:

Because I have _____ , I will give _____ .

Day _____

Today I am grateful for:

1. _____

2. _____

3. _____

Today's intention:

```



```

Because I have _____ , I will give _____

Day _____

Today I am grateful for:

1. _____

2. _____

3. _____

Today's intention:

Because I have _____ , I will give _____

Day _____

Today I am grateful for:

1. _____

2. _____

3. _____

Today's intention:

Because I have _____ , I will give _____

Day _____

Today I am grateful for:

1. _____

2. _____

3. _____

Today's intention:

[ ]

Because I have _____, I will give _____.

Day _____

Today I am grateful for:

1. _____

2. _____

3. _____

Today's intention:

Because I have _____ , I will give _____

Day _____

Today I am grateful for:

1. _____

2. _____

3. _____

Today's intention:

_____

Because I have _____ , I will give _____ .

Day _____

Today I am grateful for:

1. _____

2. _____

3. _____

Today's intention:

```



```

Because I have _____, I will give _____

Day _____

Today I am grateful for:

1. _____

2. _____

3. _____

Today's intention:

Because I have _____ , I will give _____ .

Day _____

Today I am grateful for:

1. _____

2. _____

3. _____

Today's intention:

Because I have _____, I will give _____

Day _____

Today I am grateful for:

1. _____

2. _____

3. _____

Today's intention:

Because I have _____, I will give _____

Day _____

Today I am grateful for:

1. _____

2. _____

3. _____

Today's intention:

┌───┐
│   │
│   │
│   │
│   │
│   │
│   │
│   │
└───┘

Because I have _____ , I will give _____

Day _____

Today I am grateful for:

1. _____

2. _____

3. _____

Today's intention:

Because I have _____, I will give _____

Day _____

Today I am grateful for:

1. _____

2. _____

3. _____

Today's intention:

Because I have _____ , I will give _____

Day _____

Today I am grateful for:

1. _____

2. _____

3. _____

Today's intention:

Because I have _____ , I will give _____ .

Day _____

Today I am grateful for:

1. _____

2. _____

3. _____

Today's intention:

_____

Because I have _____ , I will give _____

Day _____

Today I am grateful for:

1. _____

2. _____

3. _____

Today's intention:

_____
| |
| |
| |
| |
| |
| |
|_____|

Because I have _____ , I will give _____

Day _____

Today I am grateful for:

1. _____

2. _____

3. _____

Today's intention:

Because I have _____ , I will give _____

Day _____

Today I am grateful for:

1. _____

2. _____

3. _____

Today's intention:

Because I have _____, I will give _____.

Day _____

Today I am grateful for:

1. _____

2. _____

3. _____

Today's intention:

Because I have _____ , I will give _____ .

Day _____

Today I am grateful for:

1. _____

2. _____

3. _____

Today's intention:

Because I have _____, I will give _____

Day _____

Today I am grateful for:

1. _____

2. _____

3. _____

Today's intention:

_____

Because I have _____ , I will give _____ .

Day _____

Today I am grateful for:

1. _____

2. _____

3. _____

Today's intention:

```
┌─────────────────────────────────────────────┐
│                                               │
│                                               │
│                                               │
│                                               │
│                                               │
│                                               │
│                                               │
└─────────────────────────────────────────────┘
```

Because I have _____, I will give _____

Day _____

Today I am grateful for:

1. _____

2. _____

3. _____

Today's intention:

Because I have _____, I will give _____

Day _____

Today I am grateful for:

1. _____

2. _____

3. _____

Today's intention:

Because I have _____ , I will give _____

Day _____

Today I am grateful for:

1. _____

2. _____

3. _____

Today's intention:

┌──┐
│   │
│   │
│   │
│   │
│   │
│   │
└──┘

Because I have _____ , I will give _____

Day _____

Today I am grateful for:

1. _____

2. _____

3. _____

Today's intention:

```

```

Because I have _____ , I will give _____ .

Day _____

Today I am grateful for:

1. _____

2. _____

3. _____

Today's intention:

```



```

Because I have _____, I will give _____

Day _____

Today I am grateful for:

1. _____

2. _____

3. _____

Today's intention:

Because I have _____ , I will give _____

Day _____

Today I am grateful for:

1. _____

2. _____

3. _____

Today's intention:

Because I have _____ , I will give _____

Day _____

Today I am grateful for:

1. _____

2. _____

3. _____

Today's intention:

Because I have _____ , I will give _____

Day _____

Today I am grateful for:

1. _____

2. _____

3. _____

Today's intention:

```
┌─────────────────────────────────────────────────┐
│                                                   │
│                                                   │
│                                                   │
│                                                   │
│                                                   │
│                                                   │
└─────────────────────────────────────────────────┘
```

Because I have _____ , I will give _____

Day _____

Today I am grateful for:

1. _____

2. _____

3. _____

Today's intention:

Because I have _____ , I will give _____

Day _____

Today I am grateful for:

1. _____

2. _____

3. _____

Today's intention:

Because I have _____ , I will give _____

Day _____

Today I am grateful for:

1. _____

2. _____

3. _____

Today's intention:

+--+
| |
| |
| |
| |
| |
| |
| |
+--+

Because I have _____, I will give _____

Day _____

Today I am grateful for:

1. _____

2. _____

3. _____

Today's intention:

Because I have _____ , I will give _____

Day _____

Today I am grateful for:

1. _____

2. _____

3. _____

Today's intention:

```
┌─────────────────────────────────────────────┐
│                                               │
│                                               │
│                                               │
│                                               │
│                                               │
│                                               │
│                                               │
└─────────────────────────────────────────────┘
```

Because I have _____ , I will give _____

Day _____

Today I am grateful for:

1. _____

2. _____

3. _____

Today's intention:

[ ]

Because I have _____ , I will give _____

Day _____

Today I am grateful for:

1. _____

2. _____

3. _____

Today's intention:

Because I have _____ , I will give _____ .

Day _____

Today I am grateful for:

1. _____

2. _____

3. _____

Today's intention:

```
┌────────────────────────────────────────────────┐
│                                                  │
│                                                  │
│                                                  │
│                                                  │
│                                                  │
│                                                  │
│                                                  │
└────────────────────────────────────────────────┘
```

Because I have _____ , I will give _____

Day _____

Today I am grateful for:

1. _____

2. _____

3. _____

Today's intention:

```
┌─────────────────────────────────────────────────┐
│                                                   │
│                                                   │
│                                                   │
│                                                   │
│                                                   │
│                                                   │
│                                                   │
└─────────────────────────────────────────────────┘
```

Because I have _____, I will give _____

Day _____

Today I am grateful for:

1. _____

2. _____

3. _____

Today's intention:

_____
| |
| |
| |
| |
| |
| |
| |
| |
|_____|

Because I have _____ , I will give _____

Day _____

Today I am grateful for:

1. _____

2. _____

3. _____

Today's intention:

[ ]

Because I have _____ , I will give _____

Day _____

Today I am grateful for:

1. _____

2. _____

3. _____

Today's intention:

Because I have _____ , I will give _____

Day _____

Today I am grateful for:

1. _____

2. _____

3. _____

Today's intention:

Because I have _____ , I will give _____

Day _____

Today I am grateful for:

1. _____

2. _____

3. _____

Today's intention:

Because I have _____ , I will give _____ .

Day _____

Today I am grateful for:

1. _____

2. _____

3. _____

Today's intention:

```



```

Because I have _____ , I will give _____

Day _____

Today I am grateful for:

1. _____

2. _____

3. _____

Today's intention:

```
┌─────────────────────────────────────────────┐
│                                               │
│                                               │
│                                               │
│                                               │
│                                               │
│                                               │
│                                               │
│                                               │
└─────────────────────────────────────────────┘
```

Because I have _____, I will give _____

Day _____

Today I am grateful for:

1. _____

2. _____

3. _____

Today's intention:

Because I have _____ , I will give _____ .

Day _____

Today I am grateful for:

1. _____

2. _____

3. _____

Today's intention:

```




```

Because I have _____, I will give _____.

Day _____

Today I am grateful for:

1. _____

2. _____

3. _____

Today's intention:

Because I have _____ , I will give _____ .

Day _____

Today I am grateful for:

1. _____

2. _____

3. _____

Today's intention:

Because I have _____ , I will give _____

Day _____

Today I am grateful for:

1. _____

2. _____

3. _____

Today's intention:

```


```

Because I have _____, I will give _____

Day _____

Today I am grateful for:

1. _____

2. _____

3. _____

Today's intention:

[ ]

Because I have _____ , I will give _____

Day _____

Today I am grateful for:

1. _____

2. _____

3. _____

Today's intention:

```




```

Because I have _____ , I will give _____ .

Day _____

Today I am grateful for:

1. _____

2. _____

3. _____

Today's intention:

Because I have _____, I will give _____

Day _____

Today I am grateful for:

1. _____

2. _____

3. _____

Today's intention:

┌─────────────────────────────────────┐
│   │
│   │
│   │
│   │
│   │
│   │
└─────────────────────────────────────┘

Because I have _____ , I will give _____ .

Day _____

Today I am grateful for:

1. _____

2. _____

3. _____

Today's intention:

Because I have _____ , I will give _____.

Day _____

Today I am grateful for:

1. _____

2. _____

3. _____

Today's intention:

```
┌─────────────────────────────────────────┐
│                                           │
│                                           │
│                                           │
│                                           │
│                                           │
│                                           │
│                                           │
└─────────────────────────────────────────┘
```

Because I have _____ , I will give _____

Day _____

Today I am grateful for:

1. _____

2. _____

3. _____

Today's intention:

Because I have _____ , I will give _____ .

Day _____

Today I am grateful for:

1. _____

2. _____

3. _____

Today's intention:

```



```

Because I have _____ , I will give _____.

Day _____

Today I am grateful for:

1. _____

2. _____

3. _____

Today's intention:

Because I have _____ , I will give _____ .

Day _____

Keep in touch:

@alex_elle on instagram

@_alexelle on twitter